In The Year 1918

By

Kerry Butters

Contents

Timeline / News
January

Jan 1 Last day of the Julian calendar in Finland

Jan 1 4th Rose Bowl: Mare Island - USMC beats Camp Lewis - US Army 19-7

Jan 2 Dodgers trade Casey Stengel & Cutshaw to Pitts for Grimes & Mamaux

Jan 2 NHL Montreal Wanderers disband after Westmount arena burns down

Jan 3 US Employment Service opens as a unit of the Department of Labor

Jan 5 British premier Lloyd George demand for unified peace

Jan 8 Mississippi becomes 1st state to ratify 18th amendment (prohibition of alcohol) of the US Constitution

Jan 8 US President Woodrow Wilson outlines his Fourteen Points for peace after the Great War

Jan 12 Montreal Canadien Joe Malone scores 5 goals beating Ottawa 9-4 Ice Hockey Player Joe Malone

Jan 12 Finland's "Mosaic Confessors" law went into effect, making Finnish Jews full citizens.

Jan 14 Finland and USSR adopt New Style (Gregorian) calendar

Jan 16 Austria and Germany are disrupted by strikes as people express impatience with leaders continuing the war

Jan 19 Soviets disallow a Constitution Assembly

Jan 19 Finnish Civil War: The first serious battles between the Red Guards and the White Guard

Jan 22 Ukraine proclaimed a free republic

Jan 25 Russia declared a republic of Soviets

Jan 26 Herbert Hoover, US Food Administrator, calls for "wheatless" & "meatless" days for war effort

Jan 27 "Tarzan of the Apes", 1st Tarzan film, premieres at Broadway Theater
Jan 27 The first hostilities occurred in the Finnish Civil War.

Jan 28 Strike on Berlin ammunition factory
Jan 28 Finnish Civil War: Rebels seized control of the capital, Helsinki, and members of the Senate of Finland go underground.

Jan 29 Ukrainian-Soviet War: Battle of Kruty

Jan 31 A series of accidental collisions on a misty Scottish night leads to the loss of two Royal Navy submarines with over a hundred lives, and damage to another five British warships.

February
Feb 1 Franz Lehar's opera "Wo die Lerche singt" premieres in Budapest
Feb 1 Jerome Kern, Guy Bolton & P. G. Wodehouse's musical premieres in New York
Feb 1 Russia adopts the Gregorian calendar (making the day February 14)

Feb 3 Twin Peaks Tunnel for streetcars begins service in San Francisco, at 11,920 feet one of world's longest

Feb 5 1st US pilot to down an enemy airplane, Stephen W. Thompson
Feb 5 Separation of church and state begins in USSR

Feb 6 Great Britain grants women (30 & over) the vote

Feb 8 "Stars & Stripes weekly US armed forces newspaper, 1st published

Feb 9 US Army chaplain school organizes at Ft Monroe, Virginia
Feb 9 Sacha Guitry's "Deburan" premieres in Paris

Feb 10 Trotsky declares that Russia is leaving the war
Feb 10 In Finland, General Carl G. Von Mannerheim gathers an army known as the 'White Guard' to mount a counter revolution against the Bolshevik 'Red Guard'

Feb 11 US President Woodrow Wilson makes another speech before Congress and announces 'the Four Principles' - freedom of navigation, and end to secret diplomacy, and similar items - that supplement his Fourteen Points

Feb 14 H Atteridge & S Rombergs musical "Sinbad," premieres in NYC
Feb 14 USSR adopts New Style (Gregorian) calendar (originally Feb 1)

Feb 15 US army troop ship torpedoed & sunk by Germany off Ireland
Feb 15 Estonia, Latvia & Lithuania adopt Gregorian calendar

Feb 16 Lithuania declares independence from Russia & Germany (National Day)

Feb 18 Germany renews its offensive against the Russians, making dramatic gains against disorganized and dispirited Russian troops

Feb 21 Australians chase Turkish troop out of Jericho, Dutch Palestine
Feb 21 The last Carolina parakeet dies in captivity at the Cincinnati Zoo

Feb 22 Germany claims Baltic states, Finland & Ukraine from Russia

Feb 23 First victory of Red Army over the Kaiser's German troops near Narva and Pskov. Since 1923 this date become the Day of Red Army in honour of this victory.

Feb 24 Estonia declares independence from Russia

Feb 26 Stands at Hong Kong Jockey Club collapse & burn, killing 604

March
Mar 2 NY Yankees purchase 1st baseman George Burns from Detroit Tigers & immediately trades him to Philadelphia A's

Mar 3 Richard Goering's "Seeschlacht" premieres in Berlin
Mar 3 Facing internal counterrevolutionary pressures and external German offensive, Bolsheviks forced to sign harsh Treaty of Brest-Litovsk with Germany and Austria

Mar 4 Terek Autonomous Republic established in RSFSR (until 1921)
Mar 4 First recorded case of Spanish flu at Funston Army Camp, Kanas; start of worldwide pandemic killing 50-100 million

Mar 6 US naval boat "Cyclops" disappears in Bermuda Triangle

Mar 7 H Carroll & J McCarthy's musical "Oh, Look!" premieres in NYC
Mar 7 President Woodrow Wilson authorizes US Army's Distinguished Service Medal
Mar 7 World War I: Finland forms an alliance with Germany

Mar 9 Russian Bolshevik Party becomes the Communist Party
Mar 9 Ukrainian mobs massacre Jews of Seredino Buda
Mar 9 Wageningen Agricultural College Neth opens

Mar 11 Moscow becomes capital of revolutionary Russia
Mar 11 Save the Redwoods League founded
Mar 11 First confirmed cases of the Spanish Flu in the US are reported at Fort Riley, Kansas

Mar 13 Trotsky gains control of the Red Army

Mar 13 American Red Magen David (Jewish Red Cross) forms

Mar 13 1st NHL championship: Montreal Canadiens beat Toronto Arenas, outscoring them 10-7 in a 2 game set

Mar 14 1st concrete ship to cross the Atlantic (Faith) is launched in San Francisco

Mar 16 Geoffrey O'Hara's "K-K-K-Katy" song published

Mar 17 US Ladies' Figure Skating championship won by Rosemary Beresford

Mar 17 US Men's Figure Skating championship won by Nathaniel Niles

Mar 18 Soccer team SON OF Meerssen forms

Mar 18 Socialist Youth AJC organizes in Amsterdam

Mar 19 US Congress authorizes time zones & approves daylight saving time

Mar 19 S Potter becomes 1st US pilot to shoot down a German seaplane

Mar 21 -28] During WW I Germany launches Somme offensive

Mar 23 Alick Wickham dives 200' into Australia's Yarra River

Mar 23 Crépy-en-Laonnoise: German artillery shells Paris, 256 killed

Mar 23 Lithuania proclaims independence

Mar 23 Paris bombs "Thick Bertha's Dike" (nickname for the widow Krupp)

Mar 23 German forces advance 14 miles to the Somme River (WW1)

Mar 25 The Belarusian People's Republic is established.

Mar 27 Moldova and Bessarabia join Romania

Mar 30 Stanley Cup: Toronto Arenas (NHL) beat Vancouver

Millionaires (PCHA), 3 games to 2

Mar 31 1st daylight savings time in US goes into effect

April
Apr 1 Henry Miller's Theater opens at 124 W 43rd St NYC
Apr 1 United Kingdom: the Royal Air Force is created from the Royal
Naval Air Service and the Royal Flying Corps.

Apr 3 US House of Representatives accepts American Creed written by
William Tyler

Apr 4 Food riot in Amsterdam

Apr 9 Latvia proclaims independence

Apr 13 Electrical fire kills 38 mental patients at Oklahoma State
Hospital

Apr 14 Douglas Campbell is 1st US ace pilot (shooting down 5th
German plane)

Apr 15 Georges Clémenceau publishes secret French/Austrian
documents

Apr 16 The British House of Commons passes a new Military Service
Bill, taking men up to 55 years old and extending to Ireland

Apr 18 Cleveland center fielder Tris Speaker turns an unassisted double
play

Apr 20 Manfred von Richthofen, aka The Red Baron, shoots down his
79th and 80th victims marking his final victories before his death the
following day

Apr 21 World War I: German fighter ace Baron Manfred von Richthofen "The Red Baron", shot down and killed over Vaux sur Somme in France, Canadian pilot Arthur Roy Brown credited with the kill

Apr 23 Battle of Zeebrugge ends
Apr 23 Dover Patrol overthrows Germany U-boat in East Sea
Apr 23 National Urban League forms

Apr 27 Giants' 9-0 winning start & Dodgers' 0-9 losing streak are stopped

Apr 29 Tris Speaker ties career outfield record of 4 unassisted double plays

Apr 30 Orange Nassau soccer team forms in Groningen

May
May 2 General Motors acquires the Chevrolet Motor Company of Delaware.

May 4 Yankees set record with 8 sacrifices, beat Red Sox's Babe Ruth 5-4

May 10 HMS Vindictive sunk to block entrance of Ostend Harbor

May 11 44th Kentucky Derby: William Knapp on Exterminator wins in 2:10.8

May 13 1st US airmail stamps issued (24 cents)

May 14 Sunday baseball is made legal in Washington, DC

May 15 1st regular US airmail postal service between NY, Philadelphia & Washington, D.C.
May 15 43rd Preakness: Johnny Loftus aboard War Cloud wins in

1:53.6

May 15 Greeks troops land at Smyrna

May 15 Washington Senator Walter Johnson pitches 1-0, 18 inning game

May 15 The Finnish Civil War ends

May 16 The Sedition Act of 1918 is passed by the U.S. Congress, making criticism of the government an imprisonable offense.

May 18 Dutch Indian Volksraad installed in Batavia

May 18 TNT explosion in chemical factory in Oakdale, Pennsylvania, kills 200

May 19 Wash 1st Sunday game, Senators beat Cleveland 1-0 in 18 innings

May 20 1st electrically propelled warship (New Mexico)

May 21 US House of Representatives passes amendment allowing women to vote

May 23 King Oil/Shell refinery on Curacao officially opens

May 24 Cleveland Indians Stan Coveleski sets club record for most innings pitched (19)

May 24 Cleveland beats Yankees 3-2 in 19th inning

May 24 British officer General Poole lands at Murmansk, the Russian port on the Barents Sea

May 26 Georgian Social Democratic Republic declares independence from Russia

May 26 Armenia defeats the Ottoman Army in the Battle of Sardarapat

May 27 Third Battle of Aisne: German offensive overcomes British forces (WWI)

May 28 Azerbaijan gains independence and declares itself a Democratic Republic

June

Jun 1 Excelsior Maassluis soccer team forms in Maassluis

Jun 1 White Sox losing 5-4 against NY Yankees, load the bases in 9th with no outs Chick Gandil lines to Frank Baker who turns a triple play

Jun 1 Canadian ace Billy Bishop downs 6 aircrafts over a three-day span, including German ace Paul Bilik, reclaiming his top scoring title from James McCudden

Jun 3 US Supreme Court in Hammer v. Dagenhart rules child labor laws unconstitutional

Jun 4 French troops, with the aid of US troops, stop the Germans at Chateau-Thierry as they attempt to cross the Marne

Jun 6 Battle of Belleau Wood, 1st US victory of WW I

Jun 8 Nova Aquila, brightest nova since Kepler's nova of 1604, discovered

Jun 12 1st aerial bombing raid by an American unit, France

Jun 13 Phillies and Cards tie 8-8 in 19 innings

Jun 15 1" of snow falls in Northern Pennsylvania

Jun 22 Circus train rammed by troop train kills 68 (Ivanhoe, Illinois)

Jun 22 32nd U.S. Women's National Championship: Molla Bjurstedt beats Eleanor Goss (6-4, 6-3)

Jun 23 Boston Red Sox Dutch Leonard's 2nd no-hitter beats Tigers, 5-0

Jun 25 Baku-Turkish communist party forms

Jun 26 The Australian steamer Wimmera is sunk by a mine laid north of Cape Maria van Diemen in 1917 by the German raider Wolf; 26 of its 151 passengers and crew were killed

Jun 28 1st flight between Hawaiian Islands

Jun 29 A provisional government opposed to the Bolsheviks establishes itself at Vladivostok, the Russian port on the Sea of Japan

Jun 30 Prominent US Socialist and Pacifist Eugene Debs is arrested on charges of denouncing the government, a violation of the Espionage Act of 1917

July
Jul 3 SDAP'er Suze Groenweg elected 1st woman in Dutch parliament

Jul 4 Altar dedicated at full-scale replica of Stonehenge at Maryhill, Washington
Jul 4 Ottoman sultan Mehmed VI ascends to the throne

Jul 8 Babe Ruth's blast over the fence in Fenway scores Amos Strunk, the Red Sox win 1-0 over Cleve, prevailing rules reduce Babe's HR to a triple

Jul 9 101 killed and 171 injured in worst US train wreck, Nashville, Tennessee
Jul 9 US Congress creates Distinguished Service Medal (not to be confused with other countries' decorations of the same name)

Jul 10 Russian Soviet Federal Socialist Republic forms

Jul 12 Japanese battleship explodes in Bay of Tokayama, 500 killed

Jul 14 Dutch government reclaims South seas

Jul 15 World War I: Second Battle of Marne begins

Jul 17 Longest errorless game, Cubs beat Phillies 2-1 in 21 innings
Jul 17 The Romanov royal family and several of their retainers are executed by a Bolshevik firing squad in the basement of Ipatiev House, in Yekaterinburg, Siberia

Jul 18 World War I: US and French forces launch Aisne-Marne offensive

Jul 19 World War I: German armies retreat across Marne River in France
Jul 19 Wash catcher Eddie Ainsmith applies for deferment from the draft Secretary of War Newton D Baker rules baseball players are not draft exempt

Jul 21 U-156 shells Nauset Beach, in Orleans, Massachusetts.

Jul 22 Lightning kills 504 sheep in Utah's Wasatch National Park

Jul 25 Annette Adams sworn in as 1st woman district attorney of US, California
Jul 25 Race riot in Chester Pennsylvania (3 blacks and 2 whites killed)

Jul 26 Race riot in Philadelphia (3 whites & 1 black killed)

Jul 27 Socony 200, 1st concrete barge in US, launched to carry oil, NY

August
Aug 1 British troops enter Vladivostok
Aug 1 Pittsburgh Pirates beat Boston Braves, 2-0, in 21 innings

Aug 2 Japan announces that it is deploying troops to Siberia in the aftermath of World War I

Aug 3 The first allied troops land at Archangel, the Russian port on the White Seas

Aug 4 Adolf Hitler receives the Iron Cross first class for bravery on the recommendation of his Jewish superior, Lieutenant Hugo Gutmann

Aug 6 Ferdinand Foch becomes Marshal of France during WWI
Aug 6 World War I: Second Battle of the Marne ends

Aug 8 World War I: The Allies launch the Hundred Days Offensive, beginning with the Battle of Amiens where 500 tanks and 10 Allied divisions attacked German lines
Aug 8 6 US soldiers surrounded by Germans in France, Alvin York given command, shoots 20 Germans and captures 132 more

Aug 9 Reds manager Christy Mathewson suspects Hal Chase of taking bribes to fix games, and suspends him "for indifferent play"

Aug 12 WWI: Allies defeat Germans at the Battle of Amiens - the last great battle on the Western Front

Aug 13 Bayerische Motoren Werke AG (BMW) established as a public company in Germany

Aug 15 1st full length cartoon (Sinking of Lusitania)

Aug 16 US troops overrun at Archangelsk by Bolshevik troops

Aug 17 British troops attack Baku, Azerbaijan
Aug 17 Samuel Riddle buys Man o'War for $5,000
Aug 17 Turkish troops overthrow Caukasus
Aug 17 Bolshevik revolutionary leader Moisei Uritsky is assassinated

Aug 19 Irving Berlin's musical "Yip Yip Yaphank" premieres in NYC

Aug 20 WWI: Britain opens offensive on Western front

Aug 24 Chicago Cubs, win earliest pennent ever (season ended Sept 2)
Aug 24 Sect Baker grants extended exemption to World Series players

Aug 26 W Smith & F Bacon's "Lightnin'" premieres in NYC

Aug 27 Christy Mathewson resigns as Reds manager to accept a
commission as a captain in chemical warfare branch of Army
Aug 27 Dr Joseph L Johnson named as US minister to Liberia

Aug 28 Tris Speaker suspended for season due to assault on umpire Tom
Connolly

Aug 29 Bapaume taken by Australian Corps and Canadian Corps in the
Hundred Days Offensive

Aug 30 Czechoslovakia forms independent republic
Aug 30 Fanya Kaplan attempts but fails to assassinate Lenin, new leader
of Soviet Russia

Aug 31 Boston Red Sox, win earliest AL pennent ever (season ended

September
Sep 1 Baseball season ends due to WW I
Sep 1 Ty Cobb pitches 2 innings against Browns
Sep 1 US troops land in Vladivostok, Siberia, stay until 1920

Sep 3 5 soldiers hanged for alleged participation in Houston riot (or
Camp Logan riot); in all 19 mutineers were executed.
Sep 3 Allies forced Germans back across Hindenburg Line
Sep 3 38th U.S. Men's National Tennis Championship: Robert Lindley
Murray beats Bill Tilden (6-3, 6-1, 7-5)

Sep 4 Jhr Ch Ruys de Beerenbrouck becomes 1st Dutch Catholic premier

Sep 4 US troops land in Archangel, Russia, stay 10 months

Sep 5 Due to WW I, 15th World Series begins a month early

Sep 5 Decree "On Red Terror" is published in Russia

Sep 9 Dutch government of Ruijs de Beerenbrouck forms

Sep 10 Players on both sides threaten to strike the World Series unless they are guaranteed $2,500 to the winners & $1,000 each for the losers

Sep 11 Boston Red Sox beat Chicago Cubs, 4 games to 2 in 15th World Series

Sep 12 WWI: US forces launch an attack on German-occupied St Mihiel

Sep 13 Train accident at Weesp Neth, kills 42

Sep 14 WWI: Austria-Hungary sends a note to the Allies requesting peace discussions, but the Allies reject the offer

Sep 18 Battle of Megiddo (Palestine) starts

Sep 20 Royal Dutch Blast furnace & Steel factory opens in Hague

Sep 26 Beginning of the Meuse-Argonne Offensive, more than 1 million American soldiers in the largest and most costly offensive of WWI

Sep 29 WWI: Allied forces scored a decisive breakthrough of Hindenburg Line

October
Oct 1 World War I: Arab forces under T. E. Lawrence ("Lawrence of Arabia") capture Damascus

Oct 3 Boris becomes king of Bulgaria

Oct 3 Tsar Ferdinand I of Bulgaria abdicates the throne in favour of his eldest son Tsar Boris III

Oct 3 Selwyn Theater opens at 229 W 42nd St NYC

Oct 4 Musical "Sometime" with Mae West premieres in NYC

Oct 6 US ship Otranto sinks between Scotland & Ireland, 425 die

Oct 8 American soldier Alvin York single-handedly attacks German gun nest, killing 25 and capturing 132 Germans

Oct 10 Baden's Geisz forms government

Oct 11 Major tsumani shakes Caribbean

Oct 12 Cloquet fire kills 453 and injures or displaces 52,000 people

Oct 15 British Q-ship Cymric sinks British submarine J6

Oct 17 De Kooy airport in Netherlands opens

Oct 17 Yugoslavia proclaims itself a republic

Oct 18 Czechoslovakia declares independence from Austro-Hungarian Empire

Oct 18 NHL's Quebec Bulldogs sold to a Toronto businessman P. J. Quinn

Oct 18 Russian 10th Army drives out White armies of Tsaritsyn (Stalingrad)

Oct 20 In order to secure an armistice, Germany agrees to further concessions

Oct 21 Margaret Owen sets world typing speed record of 170 wpm for 1 min

Oct 25 Canadian steamship "Princess Sophia" hits a reef off Alaska, 398 die

Oct 26 Cecil Chubb gives prehistoric monument Stonehenge to the British nation
Oct 26 Soldiers revolt at Harskamp, Veluwe
Oct 26 Germany's supreme commander General Eric Ludendorff resigns, protesting the terms to which the German Government has agreed in negotiating an armistice

Oct 28 Czechoslovakia gains independence as Austria-Hungary breaks up

Oct 29 German sailors refuse to obey orders to fight British naval forces and lead a revolt in the naval ports of Wilhelmshaven, beginning the German Revolution

Oct 30 Slovakia asks for creation of Czechoslovakian state
Oct 30 WWI: Turkey signs an armistice with the Allies, agreeing to end hostilities at noon on 31 October

Oct 31 Spanish flu-virus kills 21,000 in US in 1 week
Oct 31 Short-lived Banat Republic founded in territory where Romania, Hungary and Serbia meet

November
Nov 1 102 die in a NYC BMT subway derailment at Malbone Street Brooklyn
Nov 1 Yugoslav battleship Viribus Unitis sunk by Italians

Nov 3 Austro-Hungarian Empire dissolves
Nov 3 Poland proclaims independence from Russia after WW I
Nov 3 Thousands of revolutionary German sailors with the fleet at Kiel mutiny, seize the city, and set up councils of workers and sailors

Nov 4 The Allied armistice with Austria-Hungary, signed 3 November, goes into effect

Nov 6 Republic of Poland proclaimed
Nov 6 Supreme commander of the army Gen Cutters resigns
Nov 6 WWI: On the Western Front, Germany is now retreating as French and American troops cross the Meuse and move to take Sedan

Nov 7 Robert Goddard demonstrates tube-launched solid propellant rockets
Nov 7 United Press erroneously reports WW I armistice had been signed
Nov 7 Vladimir Mayakovsky's "Misteriya Buff" premieres in Petrograd
Nov 7 The 1918 influenza epidemic spreads to Western Samoa, killing 7,542 (about 20% of the population) by the end of the year
Nov 7 Kurt Eisner overthrows the Wittelsbach dynasty in the Kingdom of Bavaria as a revolutionary uprising spreads throughout Germany

Nov 8 Pro-German supreme commander general Cutters lay-offs

Nov 9 Emperor Wilhelm II abdicates after German defeat in World War I
Nov 9 Following the collapse of Germany in World War I, the Weimar Republic of Germany is proclaimed

Nov 10 German Emperor Wilhelm II flees to Netherlands
Nov 10 Independence of Poland proclaimed by Józef Pilsudski
Nov 10 Western Union Cable Office in North Sydney, Nova Scotia receives a top-secret coded message from Europe stating on November 11, 1918 all fighting would cease on land, sea and in the air

Nov 11 Dutch SDAP leader Troelstra announces revolution
Nov 11 Emperor Charles I of Austria abdicates
Nov 11 Poland declares independence
Nov 11 Armistice signed by the Allies and Germany comes into effect and World War I hostilities end at 11am, "the eleventh hour of the

eleventh day of the eleventh month"

Nov 12 Emperor Karl of Austria-Hungary abdicates, Austria becomes a republic

Nov 13 Prince Friedrich, last reigning Prince of Waldeck and Pyrmont, abdicates
Nov 13 Russia cancels Treaty of Brest-Litovsk
Nov 13 Stahlhelm forms (anti communist/Polish/French) in Magdenburg

Nov 14 Republic of Czechoslovakia created with Tomáš Masaryk as its 1st president

Nov 16 Hungarian People's Republic declared

Nov 17 Social Democratic Party becomes Communistc Party Holland: CPH
Nov 17 German troops evacuate Brussels

Nov 18 Latvia declares independence from Russia
Nov 18 Belgian troops re-enter Brussels, lost to the German invaders on 20 August 1914

Nov 21 2 German ammunition trains explode in Hamont Belgium, 1,750 die
Nov 21 Polish soldiers organize a pogrom against Jews of Galicia, Poland
Nov 21 The German High Seas Fleet of 5 battlecruisers, 9 battleships, 7 cruisers and 49 destroyers surrendered to the British Grand Fleet and were shepherded into the Firth of Forth

Nov 22 Grand Duke Frederik II, the last Grand Duke of Baden, resigns
Nov 22 King Albert I's triumphant procession through Brussels
Nov 22 Marshal Józef Pilsudski becomes 1st President (dictator) of Poland

Nov 22 Polish forces attack Jewish community of Lemberg (Lvov)

Nov 24 Béla Can forms Hungarian Communist Party

Nov 26 The Podgorica Assembly votes for "union of the people", declaring assimilation into the Kingdom of Serbia

Nov 28 Kaiser Wilhelm II of Prussia & Germany abdicates
Nov 28 Bucovina voted for the union with the Kingdom of Romania

Nov 29 Serbia annexes Montenegro

December
Dec 1 Danish parliament passed an act to grant Iceland independence under Danish crown
Dec 1 Serbian-Croatian-Slovic kingdom proclaimed in Belgrade
Dec 1 Yugoslavia declares independence; monarchy established

Dec 4 US President Woodrow Wilson sails for Versailles Peace Conference in France, 1st President to travel outside US while in office

Dec 5 Oil refinery on Curacao opens

Dec 9 French troops occupies Mainz

Dec 10 John Heyder becomes president of baseball's National League for the 2nd time

Dec 13 US army of occupation crosses Rhine, enters Germany

Dec 14 Giacomo Puccini's opera "Il Trittico" premieres in NYC
Dec 14 David Loyd George's coalition Government wins a clear majority in the UK general election
Dec 14 Sinn Fein candidates win 73 of 105 Irish seats in UK general election, though all will refuse to take seats in Westminster, instead

meeting at a Dail Eireann in Dublin

Dec 15 American Jewish Congress holds its 1st meeting

Dec 16 Jack Dempsey KOs Carl Morris in 14 seconds
Dec 16 German troops evacuate Finland, give over Kiev in the Ukraine to revolutionary forces and pull back from Estonia as Bolshevik forces move in

Dec 17 A conference of workers' and soldiers' councils take control of German government in Berlin, until elections in January selects new national assembly

Dec 19 Robert Ripley began his "Believe It or Not" column (NY Globe)

Dec 20 Eugene O'Neill's "Moon of the Caribees" premieres in NYC
Dec 20 The Allies turn their attention to Bolshevik expansion in the East, landing troops in Crimea and Latvia

Dec 21 Red Sox trade Dutch Leonard, Ernie Shore & Duffy Lewis to Yankees for Ray Caldwell & Slim Love, Frank Gilhooey, Al Walters & $15,000

Dec 26 1st day of 1st-class cricket in Aust after WW I (Vic v NSW)
Dec 26 After spending Christmas with American troops in France, Wilson goes to London for preliminary discussions about the forthcoming peace conference

Dec 27 The Great Poland Uprising against the Germans begins.

Dec 30 John E Hoover decides to be called J. Edgar Hoover

Dec 31 Kid Gleason replaces Pants Rowland as White Sox manager

<u>Childrens Toys</u>

Despite the ongoing war, the lives of children throughout December were still centred around excitement for what Santa Claus would bring them on Christmas morning. Like television adverts today, children were bombarded with toy and present ideas in print form in papers and magazines in the run up to Christmas.

TOP TEN TOYS OF 1918
1.Teddy Bear
2.Erector Set (Meccano)
3.Lionel Trains
4.Lincoln Logs
5.Raggedy Ann Doll
6.Radio Flyer Wagon
7.Tinker Toys
8.Crayola Crayons 8 pack
9.Tin Toys
10.Tiddlywinks

Other popular toys included: Snap Card Game, Playing cards, marbles, checkers, chess, yoyos, wooden tops, Baseball Cards Ping Pong Jigsaw Puzzles
and dolls.

Famous Births
January
Jan 1 Willy den Ouden, Dutch swimmer, (WR 100m, 1:04.06)
Jan 1 Patrick Anthony Porteous, Scottish Victoria Cross recipient (d. 2000)

Jan 2 Willi Graf, German anti-Nazi activist (d. 1943)

Jan 6 Buddy Weed, pianist (Penthouse Party), born in Ossining, New York

Jan 7 Alessadro Natta, Italian political leader (Communist Party)
Jan 7 Colin Snedden, cricketer (Test NZ v England 1947, 0-46, did not bat)

Jan 10 Arthur Chung, President of Guyana (d. 2008)

Jan 11 Albert Weisser, composer

Jan 13 Lester Sill, pioneer music publisher/record producer
Jan 13 Stephen "Steve" Dunne, American actor (Professional Father, Shock), born in Northampton, Massachusetts (d. 1977)
Jan 13 Ted Willis, prolific English screenwriter (It's Great to be Young)
Jan 13 George "Bud" Hamilton, American film make-up artist (Westmore family), born in Los Angeles, California (d. 1973)

Jan 15 Andreas M Donner, Dutch jurist (constitutional law)
Jan 15 Gamal Abdel Nasser, President of Egypt (1954-1971)
Jan 15 João Figueiredo, President of Brazil (d. 1999)

Jan 16 Stirling Silliphant, screenwriter
Jan 16 Nel Benschop, Dutch poet (d. 2005)
Jan 16 Clem Jones, Lord Mayor of Brisbane, Australia (d. 2007)

Jan 17 Joseph Walker Barr, banker/politician

Jan 18 Adriano Mandarino Hypolito, priest
Jan 18 Ton Brandsteder, CEO/founder (Sony Nederland)
Jan 18 Gustave Gingras, French Canadian physician (d. 1996)

Jan 19 John H Johnson, American publisher (Negro Digest, Ebony, Jet)

Jan 21 Geoffrey Dawes, physiologist
Jan 21 Richard D. Winters, American war hero
Jan 21 Chichay [Amparo Robles Custodio], Filipino comedienne and actress (Bilangguang puso, Ngitngit ng pitong whistle bomb), born in Tondo, Manila (d. 1993)
Jan 21 Antonio Janigro, Italian cellist (Zagreb Soloists), born in Milan, Italy

Jan 22 Elmer Lach, Canadian ice hockey player, born in Nokomis, Saskatchewan

Jan 23 Gertrude B. Elion, American biochemist and drug researcher who developed groundbreaking leukemia and herpes drug treatments (Nobel 1988), born in NYC, New York (d. 1999)

Jan 24 Gottfried von Einem, Bern Switzerland, Austrian composer (Dantons Tod)
Jan 24 John McLiam [Williams], Canadian actor (First Blood, Sleeper, Men From Shiloh), born in Alberta, Canada (d. 1994)
Jan 24 Oral Roberts, Pontotoc County Oklahoma, American Televangelist, founder Oral Roberts College

Jan 25 Ernie Harwell, American baseball sportscaster

Jan 26 Nicolae Ceausescu, Communist dictator of Romania (1967-89), born in Scorniceşti, Romania (d. 1989)
Jan 26 Philip José Farmer, Terre Haute Indiana, American sci-fi novelist (Riverworld)

Jan 27 Elmore James, musician (Dust My Broom)
Jan 27 Skitch Henderson, orchestra leader (Tonight Show), born in Birmingham, England
Jan 27 William Seawell, United States Army Brigadier General (d. 2005)

Jan 28 Harry M Corbett, Bradford, puppeteer/entertainer (Sooty, Some People)
Jan 28 Suzanne Flon, French actress (One Deadly Summer, Moulin Rouge), born in Le Kremlin-Bicêtre, Seine (d. 2005)
Jan 28 Trevor Skeet, British MP
Jan 28 Vito Scotti [Scozarri], American actor (The Godfather, Flying Nun, Barefoot in the Park), born in San Francisco, California (d. 1996)
Jan 28 Wilson Ferreira Aldunate, Uruguayan politician/human rights worker

Jan 29 John Forsythe, actor (Bachelor Father, Charlie's Angels, Dynasty), born in Penns Grove, New Jersey (d. 2010)
Jan 29 William Rigney, baseball manager (SF Giants)

Jan 30 David Opatoshu [Opatovsky], American actor and writer (Star Trek, Bonino, Secret Empire, Masada), born in NYC, New York (d. 1996)
Jan 30 Jarl Andre Bjerke, [Bernhard Borge], Norwegian poet/writer

February
Feb 1 Maurice Laing, life president (John Laing)
Feb 1 Muriel Spark, Scottish writer (The Prime of Miss Jean Brodie), born in Edinburgh, Scotland (d. 2006)

Feb 2 Hella [S Lelyveld-]Haasse, Dutch author (Cider for Poor People)

Feb 3 Joey Bishop, [Gottlieb], talk show host (Joey Bishop Show), born in The Bronx, New York
Feb 3 Helen Stephens, Fulton Mo, American 100m runner (double

Olympic gold-1936)

Feb 4 Ida Lupino, Anglo-American actress (Adventures of Sherlock Holmes) and director (The Hitch-Hiker), born in London, England (d. 1995)
Feb 4 Norman Wisdom, comedian (Kraft Music Hall), born in London, England
Feb 4 Luigi Pareyson, Italian philosopher (d. 1991)

Feb 5 Gara Garayev [Kara Karayev], Soviet-Azerbaijani composer (Seven Beauties), born in Baku (d. 1982)

Feb 6 Lothar-Günther Buchheim, German author (d. 2007)

Feb 7 Markey Robinson, Northern Irish painter (d. 1999)

Feb 8 John Intoxication, resistance fighter
Feb 8 Lord Maxd Rayne, English broker/multi-millionaire
Feb 8 Fred Blassie, American professional wrestler (d. 2003)

Feb 10 Gordon Pirie, English Group Captain and politician, born in Oxford (d. 2003)
Feb 10 Idwal Pugh, British ombudsman

Feb 11 Margaret Heldt, American hairdresser who created the Beehive, born in Chicago, Illinois

Feb 12 Dominic DiMaggio, baseball outfielder (Boston Red Sox)
Feb 12 Julian S Schwinger, US physicist

Feb 13 Patty Berg, LPGA golfer (1938 US Amateur), born in Minneapolis, Minnesota

Feb 15 Alan Arbus, American actor and photographer (M*A*S*H, Greaser's Palace, Curb Your Enthusiasm), born in NYC, New York (d.

2013)

Feb 16 Patty Andrews, American vocalist (Andrews Sisters), born in Minneapolis, Minnesota

Feb 17 Charles A Hayes, (Rep-D-IL, 1983-)
Feb 17 Olive Gibbs, peace campaigner

Feb 18 Jane Loevinger, American psychologist (d. 2008).

Feb 20 Leonore Annenberg American Billionaire

Feb 22 Charles O Finley, baseball team owner (Oakland A's)
Feb 22 Don Pardo, Westfield Mass, TV announcer (Jeopardy, Saturday Night Live)
Feb 22 Robert Wadlow, Alton Ill, tallest known human (2.72 m, 8' 11.1")
Feb 22 Sid Abel, Melville, Saskatchewan, Canadian NHL hockey player (1948-49 Hart Trophy)
Feb 22 Charlie Finley, American sports entrepreneur (d. 1996)
Feb 22 Alfred J. Gross, American inventor (invented the walkie-talkie), born in Toronto, Canada (d. 2000)

Feb 23 Dom Aelred Watkin, headmaster (Downside School)
Feb 23 Richard G. Butler, American fascist (d. 2004)

Feb 25 Henry Norwood Ewell, 4x100m runner (Olympic gold 1948), born in Harrisburg, Pennsylvania
Feb 25 Barney Ewell, American athlete (d. 1996)
Feb 25 Rena Kyriakou, Greek pianist (d. 1994)
Feb 25 Bobby Riggs, American tennis player ("The Battle of the Sexes", US Open 1939, 41), born in Los Angeles, California (d. 1995)

Feb 26 Edwin Charles "Preacher" Roe, baseball pitcher (Bkln Dodgers)
Feb 26 Otis R Bowen, US Sec of Health & Human Services (1985-89)

Feb 26 Theodore Sturgeon, American sci-fi author (Hugo, It, Caviar), born in Staten Island, New York (d. 1985)

Feb 28 Alfred Burke, British actor (Public Eye, Backfire, Harry Potter and the Chamber of Secrets), born in London, England (d. 2011)

March
Mar 1 Roger Delgado, English actor (Doctor Who, Agent 8 3/4, Hot Enough for June), born in London, England (d. 1973)
Mar 1 Gladys Noon Spellman, American politician (d. 1988)

Mar 3 Peter O'Sullevan, British horse racing commentator 'the voice of racing', born in Kenmare, Ireland (d. 2015)
Mar 3 Arnold Newman, photographer (Faces USA)
Mar 3 Arthur Kornberg, US biochemist (Nobel 1959)
Mar 3 Frank Wigglesworth, composer
Mar 3 Fritz Thiedemann, German equestrian (d. 2000)

Mar 4 Margaret Osborne DuPont, Joseph Oregon, tennis pro (US Open 1948-50), (d. 2012)

Mar 5 Halsey S Colchester, British SAS/spy (MI6)/priest
Mar 5 Ranga Sohoni, Indian cricketer (pace bowler of late 40's avg 101)
Mar 5 Red Storey, Canadian football player and ice hockey referee (d. 2006)
Mar 5 James Tobin, American economist, Nobel laureate (d. 2002)
Mar 5 Milt Schmidt, Canadian NHL Hall of Fame center and coach (Boston Bruins), born in Kitchener, Ontario (d. 2017)

Mar 7 June Wayne, artist/lithographer/teacher

Mar 9 Marguerite Chapman, American actress (The Seven Year Itch, Spy Smasher, Flight to Mars), born in Chatham, New York (d. 1999)
Mar 9 Mickey Spillane [Frank Morrison Spillane], American mystery writer (I the Jury), born in Brooklyn, New York (d. 2006)

Mar 10 Heywood Hale Broun, TV commentator and sports correspondent, born in NYC, New York (d. 2001)
Mar 10 Günther Rall, German ace fighter pilot

Mar 12 James Bracken, race horse trainer
Mar 12 Elaine de Kooning, American artist (d. 1989)

Mar 13 George McAfee, American football player, NFL halfback (Chicago Bears), born in Corbin, Kentucky (d. 2009)

Mar 14 Dennis Patrick, American actor (Dear Dead Delilah, Dallas, Rituals), born in Philadelphia, Pennsylvania (d. 2002)

Mar 15 Janet Leach, potter, born in Grand Saline, Texas (d. 1997)
Mar 15 Richard Ellmann, American literary scholar and biographer (Oscar Wilde), born in Highland Park, Michigan (d. 1987)
Mar 15 Punch Imlach, Canadian hockey coach and general manager (d. 1987)

Mar 16 Aldo E van Eyck, Dutch architect (City Hall)
Mar 16 Howard Boatwright, composer

Mar 17 D Arendo, [Arend Honhoff], Dutch pianist/composer (Eleonora)
Mar 17 Wilhelmus M J Russell, Dutch attorney/Member of 1st chamber (KVP/CDA)

Mar 18 Al Benton, American baseball player (d. 1968)
Mar 18 Bob Broeg, American sports writer (d. 2005)
Mar 18 Yevgeny Pepelyaev, Bodaybo, Irkutsk, Soviet Union, fighter pilot, (d. 2013)

Mar 20 Bernd-Alois Zimmermann, German composer (Soldiers)
Mar 20 Jack Barry, Lindenhurst NY, game show emcee (Joker's Wild)
Mar 20 Marian McPartland, British jazz pianist (Marian McPartland's Piano Jazz), born in Slough, United Kingdom (d. 2013)

Mar 20 Donald Featherstone, British writer and wargamer

Mar 21 Joe Carveth, NHL forward (scored 20 or more goals in 3 seasons)

Mar 22 Cheddi B Jagan, dentist/founder PPP/Guyanese Premier (1953, 1957-64)
Mar 22 Harry Kay, vice-chancellor (Exeter U)
Mar 22 Tauno Kullerve Pylkkanen, composer

Mar 24 Englebert van Anderlecht, Belgian painter

Mar 25 Howard Cosell, sportscaster (Monday Night Football), born in Winston-Salem, North Carolina

Mar 28 Youly Algaroff, Russian-French ballet dancer, born in Simferopol, Crimea (d. 1995)

Mar 29 John Read, British businessman, CEO (TSB Group), born in Brighton (d. 2015)
Mar 29 Pearl Bailey, American actress and singer (Hello Dolly), born in Newport News, Virginia (d. 1990)
Mar 29 Sam Walton, American businessman (founder and CEO of Walmart and Sam's Club), born in Kingfisher, Oklahoma (d. 1992)

Mar 30 John Gray, FRS/marine biologist
Mar 30 Joseph Allen Jr, American actor (The Night Before the Divorce, Motor Madness), born in Boston, Massachusetts (d. 1962)

Mar 31 Ted Post, Dir (Peacemaker, Beneath the Planet of the Apes)

April
Apr 3 Enrique Iturriaga, Peruvian composer, born in Lima, Peru
Apr 3 Louis Applebaum, Canadian conductor and composer, born in Toronto, Canada (d. 2000)

Apr 3 Sixten Ehrling, Swedish conductor (Royal Opera of Stockholm), born in Malmö, Sweden (d. 2005)

Apr 4 George Jellicoe, Earl Jellicoe, British naval commander and member of the House of Lords (1939-2007), born in Hatfield (d. 2007)

Apr 6 Joan Bernard, Principal (Trevelyan College, Durham)
Apr 6 Karen [Ingeborg Klinkerfuss], German actress (Sky Murder, All Through the Night, Madame X), born in Berlin, Germany (d. 1967)
Apr 6 Alfredo Ovando Candía, Bolivian president (d. 1982)

Apr 7 C B Bertie Clarke, cricketer (Barbados & West Indian leg-spinner)
Apr 7 Peanuts Hucko, dixieland clarinetist (Lawrence Welk Show), born in Syracuse, New York
Apr 7 Ronald Howard, British actor (Naked Edge, Come September, Murder She Said), born in Norwood, England (d. 1996)
Apr 7 Bobby Doerr, American baseball player

Apr 8 Betty [Bloomer] Ford, US 1st lady (1974-77) and founder of the Betty Ford Center clinic, born in Chicago, Illinois (d. 2011)
Apr 8 Glendon Swarthout, American author (d. 1992)

Apr 9 Jorn Utzon, Danish architect (Sydney Opera House), born in Copenhagen, Denmark (d. 2008)

Apr 11 Jean-Claude Servan-Schreiber, journalist
Apr 11 Richard Wainwright, English politician (d. 2003)
Apr 11 William Perrie, British prison governor
Apr 12 18th earl of Derby, English landowner/multi-millionaire

Apr 13 A. L. [Audrey] Barker, English writer, born in St Pauls Cray, Kent (2002)

Apr 14 Mary Healy, American actress (The 5,000 Fingers of Dr. T, He

Married his Wife), born in New Orleans, Louisiana (d. 2016)

Apr 15 John Baragrey, American actor (Creeper, The Loves of Carmen), born in Haleyville, Alabama (d. 1975)

Apr 16 Spike Milligan, Irish-British actor and comedian (The Goon Show, 3 Musketeers), born in Ahmednagar, India (d. 2002)
Apr 16 Dick Gibson, British racing driver

Apr 17 Anne Shirley [Dawn Evelyeen Paris], British actress (The Devil and Daniel Webster, Murder My Sweet), born in NYC, New York (d. 1993)
Apr 17 William Holden [Beedle], American actor (The Blue Knight, Sunset Boulevard, Sabrina, The Bridge on the River Kwai), born in O'Fallon, Illinois (d. 1981)

Apr 18 Robert Zimonyi, Hungarian cox (Olympic-Hungary-bronze-1948/US-gold-64)
Apr 18 Roger de Grey, president (Royal Academy)
Apr 18 Tony Mottola, Kearney NJ, guitarist/host (Melody Street)
Apr 18 Cliff Hillegass, American publisher (d. 2001)

Apr 20 June Storey, Canadian-born American actress (South of the Border), born in Toronto (d. 1991)

Apr 22 Mickey Vernon, baseball player

Apr 23 Anthony Craxton, British TV producer
Apr 23 Maurice Druon, [Kessel], French writer/journalist (Prix Goncourt)
Apr 23 Gordon Hirabayshi, American civil rights activist and WWII internment opponent (Hirabayshi v. United States), born in Seattle, Washington (d. 2012)

Apr 25 Astrid Varnay, soprano (Met Opera 1941-56), born in

Stockholm, Sweden
Apr 25 Gerard Henri de Vaucouleurs, French astronomer (d. 1995)

Apr 26 Fanny Blankers-Koen, Holland, 100m/200m dash, hurdler (Olym-gold-1948)
Apr 26 Jack Morpurgo, American Literature scholar (Leeds University)
Apr 26 Stafford Repp, American actor (Playhouse 90, Batman, Plunder Road), born in San Francisco, California (d. 1974)

Apr 27 John Alfred Scali, journalist/correspondent (ABC)
Apr 27 Kirby Stone, American jazz combo leader (Baubles Bangles & Beads), born in NYC, New York
Apr 27 Willem N "Pim" Koot, pianist of Concert building (Oh, Lady! Lady!)
Apr 27 Sten Rudholm, Swedish jurist, member of the Swedish Academy

Apr 29 Mervyn Roye Harvey, cricketer (brother of Neil, Test for Australia)

Apr 30 W Donald McNeill, tennis champ (US Open-1940)

May

May 1 Jack Paar, American television host of the Jack Paar Show (d. 2004), born in Canton, Ohio
May 1 Gersh Budker, Russian physicist (d. 1977)

May 2 Frederick Archibauld Warner, diplomat

May 3 Ted Bates, English former footballer (d. 2003)

May 4 Kakuei Tanaka, Japanese PM (1972-74), convicted of bribe-taking
May 4 Thomas Mead, Australian politician and journalist (d. 2004)

May 5 Erbie Bowser, American blues and jazz pianist, born in Davila,

Texas (d. 1995)

May 6 Godfrey Ridout, composer
May 6 Sydney Chatton, England
May 6 Zayed bin Sultan Al Nahyan, 1st President of the United Arab
Emirates, born in Al Ain, Abu Dhabi, birth date disputed (d. 2004)

May 7 Argeliers Leon, composer

May 9 Mike Wallace, newscaster (Biography, 60 Minutes), born in
Brookline, Massachusetts (d. 2012)
May 9 Orville Freeman, (Sen-D-Mn)/Sec of Agriculture (1961-69), born
in Minneapolis, Minnesota

May 10 Dr. T Berry Brazelton, American child development
paediatrician, author, TV host (What Every Baby Knows), who
developed the Neonatal Behavioral Assessment Scale (NBAS), born in
Waco, Texas (d. 2018)
May 10 George Welch, American World War II flying ace (Medal of
Honor nominee) and test pilot, born in Wawaset Park, Delaware (d.
1954)

May 11 Richard P Feynman, physicist (Feynman-diagrams/Nobel prize
1965)
May 11 Robert Hunt, CEO (Dowty Group)
May 11 Richard Feynman, American theoretical physicist, born in
Queens, New York (d. 1988)

May 12 Oscar Beregi Jr, Hungarian actor (Young Frankenstein, Panic in
City), born in Budapest, Austria-Hungary (d. 1976)
May 12 Julius Rosenberg, 1st US civilian executed for espionage, born
in NYC, New York

May 13 John Johnston, British diplomat (Rhodesia, Malaysia)
May 13 T. Balasaraswati, Bharatanatyam dancer (d. 1984)

May 14 Arthur McIntyre, cricket wicket-keeper (England 3 times early 50's)

May 15 Eddy Arnold, Henderson TN, country singer (Cattle Call, Anytime)
May 15 Joseph Wiseman, Canadian actor (Dr No, Viva Zapata, Les Miserables), born in Montreal, Quebec (d. 2009)

May 16 Edward Thomas, historian/intelligence expert
May 16 Juan Rulfo, Mexican writer (Pedro Paramo)
May 16 Kevin Skelton, Bishop (Lichfield)
May 16 Wilf Mannion, English former footballer (d. 2000)

May 17 Birgit Nilsson, Karup Sweden, operatic soprano (Elektra, Salome)

May 18 Massimo Girotti, Italian actor (Last Tango in Paris, In the Name of the Law), born in Mogliano, Marche, Italy (d. 2003)

May 19 Florence Chadwick, swimmer (1st to swim English Channel both ways), born in San Diego, California (d. 1995)
May 19 Abraham Pais, Dutch-born American physicist (d. 2000)

May 20 Edward B. Lewis, American geneticist, Nobel laureate (d. 2004)

May 21 Leonard Mullens, rubber physicist

May 22 David Land, impressario

May 23 Robert "Bumps" Blackwell, band leader and record producer, born in Seattle, Washington (d. 1985)
May 23 Dennis Compton, English cricketer and footballer (5,807 runs, Arsenal), born in Middlesex, England (d. 1997)

May 24 Coleman Young, 1st African American Mayor of Detroit, born

in Tuscaloosa, Alabama
May 24 D V Jennings, solicitor

May 25 Peder Lunde, Norwegian yachtsman (Olympic silver 1952)

May 26 Anton Christoforidis, Greek boxer (d. 1985)

May 27 Yasuhiro Nakasone, premier of Japan (1982-87)

May 29 Herb Shriner, humorist/TV host (Herb Shriner Show)
May 29 Isabel Dean, English actress (Five Days One Summer Virgin Island, Ransom), born in Aldridge, Staffordshire (d. 1997)

May 30 Guadalupe "Pita" Amor, Mexican poet (d. 2000)
May 30 Bob Evans, American restaurateur (d. 2007)

June
Jun 2 Robert Manry, American copy editor of the Cleveland newspaper editor who sailed the Atlantic (Tinkerbelle), born in Landour, India (d. 1971)
Jun 2 Ruth Atkinson, American cartoonist (d. 1997)

Jun 3 Patrick Cargill, British actor (Help!, No Wreath for the General, Hammerhead), born in London, England (d. 1996)
Jun 3 Lili St. Cyr, American ecdysiast (d. 1999)

Jun 4 LeRoy Walker, CEO (US Olympic Committee), born in Atlanta, Georgia

Jun 5 Branimir Sakac, composer

Jun 6 Richard Crane,American character actor (Surfside 6, Rocky Jones, Space Ranger), born in New Castle, Indiana (d. 1969)
Jun 6 Tom Scott, poet/editor

Jun 7 Irene Vorrink, Dutch minister (health & environment)

Jun 8 Robert Preston [Meservey], American actor (Music Man, Mame, Last Starfighter), born in Newton, Massachusetts (d. 1987)
Jun 8 John D. Roberts, American chemist

Jun 9 Rob de Vries, actor and director (Ciske de Rat, Silent Raid), born in Amsterdam, Noord-Holland, Netherlands (d. 1969)

Jun 10 Herbert "Barry" Morse, British-Canadian actor (The Fugitive, Space: 1999, Winds of War), born in Shoreditch, London (d. 2009)

Jun 12 Samuel Z. Arkoff, American film producer (d. 2001)

Jun 13 Ben Johnson, American actor (Chisum, Battle Force, Dillinger), born in Foraker, Shidler, Oklahoma (d. 1996)
Jun 13 Helmut Lent, German night fighter pilot (d. 1944)

Jun 14 Carter Harman, American composer, born in Brooklyn, New York (d. 2007)
Jun 14 Leroy T Walker, US Olympic consultant (1960, 68, 72), born in Atlanta, Georgia

Jun 15 Andreas M Donner, Dutch state leader
Jun 15 N'garta Tombalbaye, president Chad

Jun 17 Maldwyn Thomas, president (Welsh Liberal Party)
Jun 17 Ajahn Chah, Buddhist meditation master (d. 1992)

Jun 18 Bob Carroll, American screen writer (I Love Lucy, Stage Two Revue, Stranger), born in McKeesport, Pennsylvania (d. 2007)

Jun 19 Evelle Jansen Younger, American prosecutor (Charles Manson, Sirhan Sirhan), born in Stamford, Nebraska (d. 1989)

Jun 20 George Lynch, American auto racer (d. 1997)
Jun 20 Zoltán Sztáray, Hungarian writer

Jun 21 James Bysse Joll, historian
Jun 21 Eddie Lopat, American baseball player (d. 1992)

Jun 22 Richard Eastham, American actor (Battle for the Planet of the Apes, Falcon Crest), born in Opelousas, Louisiana (d. 2005)
Jun 22 Cicely Saunders, English nurse, physician and writer who founded the first modern hospice, born in Barnet, England (d. 2005)

Jun 25 Ken Mayers, American actor (Little Big Man, Dick Tracey, Space Patrol), born in San Francisco, California (d. 1985)

Jun 27 Adolph Kiefer, American 100m backstroke swimmer (Olympic gold 1936), born in Chicago, Illinois (d. 2017)

Jun 28 Bert Schierbeek, [Lambertus], Dutch writer/poet (Cross Roads)

Jun 29 Jack Harkness, rose grower

Jun 30 Stuart Foster, Binghamton NY, singer (Galen Drake Show)

July
Jul 2 Sheikh Imam, Egyptian singer and composer, born in Giza (d. 1995)
Jul 2 Wibo, Dutch cartoonist (d. 2005)

Jul 3 Lord Mulley, British MP (Labour)

Jul 4 Abigail Van Buren, [Mrs Morton Phillips], Sioux City Iowa, columnist
Jul 4 Alec Bedser, cricketer (mighty post-war England medium-pacer)
Jul 4 Ann Landers, Sioux City Iowa, twin sister/advice columnist
Jul 4 Buster Davis, choral director (Garry Moore Show), born in

Johnstown, Pennsylvania
Jul 4 Eric Bedser, cricketer (bro of Alec, Surrey bowler but not England)
Jul 4 Taufa'ahau Tupou IV, King of Tonga (1965-)
Jul 4 Johnnie Parsons, American race car driver (d. 1984)
Jul 4 Pauline Phillips, Sioux City, Iowa, advice columnist (Dear Abby), (d. 2013)

Jul 5 George Rochberg, composer (Concord Quartet), born in Paterson, New Jersey

Jul 6 Bert [Lambertus H] Voeten, Dutch journalist/poet (Crossing)
Jul 6 Eugene List, American concert pianist and teacher (Eastman School of Music), born in Philadelphia, Pennsylvania
Jul 6 Sebastian Cabot, British actor (Kismet, Family Affair, Time Machine), born in London, England (d. 1977)

Jul 8 Craig Stevens [Gail Shikles Jr.], American actor (Craig-Dallas, Peter Gunn), born in Liberty, Missouri (d. 2000)

Jul 9 Herbert Brun, composer
Jul 9 Rowley I Arenstein, South African attorney/communist/ANC'er

Jul 14 Arthur Laurents, American playwright (West Side Story, Gypsy), born in NYC, New York
Jul 14 Ingmar Bergman, Swedish stage and film director (Cries & Whispers), born in Uppsala, Sweden (d. 2007)
Jul 14 Jay Forrester, Engineer, invented random-access magnetic core memory, born near Anselmo, Nebraska (d. 2016)

Jul 15 Lord Buxton of Alsa, CEO (ITV)

Jul 16 Bayani Casimiro, Filipino dancer and actor [Okey Ka Fairy Ko!], born in San Pablo, Laguna, Philippine Islands (d. 1989)
Jul 16 George Mueller, NASA Systems Engineer (managed 1969 Moon landing), born in St Louis, Missouri (d. 2015)

Jul 17 Carlos Manuel Arana Osorio, President of Guatemala (d. 2003)

Jul 18 Nelson Mandela, anti-apartheid activist, political prisoner (1962-90) and South African President (1994-99), born in Mvezo, Umtatu, South Africa (d. 2013)

Jul 20 Cindy Walker, American singer (d. 2006)

Jul 22 Pim [Albrecht W] Lyre, Dutch lawyer/son of prince Henry

Jul 23 Pee Wee [Harold] Reese, American baseball player (Dodgers), born in Ekron, Kentucky (d. 1999)

Jul 24 Ruggiero Ricci, composer/violinist (Paganini), born in San Francisco, California (d. 2012)

Jul 25 Nan Grey [Eschal Miller], American actress (Three Smart Girls, Dracula's Daughters), born in Houston, Texas (d. 1993)
Jul 25 Jane Frank, American artist (d. 1986)

Jul 26 Marjorie Lord [Wollenberg], American actress (Make Room for Daddy, Sherlock Holmes in Washington), born in San Francisco, California (d. 2015)

Jul 27 Eero Aukusti Sipila, composer
Jul 27 Leonard Rose, concert cellist (NY Phil 1943-51), born in Washington, D.C.

Jul 29 Vladimir Dudentzev, Russian writer

Jul 30 Joe Daley, jazz tenor/clarinet/flute player

Jul 31 Paul D. Boyer, American biochemist and Nobel Prize Laureate, born in Provo, Utah
Jul 31 Hank Jones, American jazz pianist and composer, born in The

Bronx, New York (d. 2010)

August

Aug 1 Wyndraeth Morris-Jones, British political scientist, born in Carmarthenshire (d. 1999)

Aug 3 Jordan Whitfield, American actor (Bomba the Jungle Boy, Lord of the Jungle, Swamp Fox), born in Pittsburgh, Pennsylvania (d. 1967)
Aug 3 James MacGregor Burns, political writer (The Lion & the Fox)
Aug 3 Sidney Gottlieb, American CIA official (d. 1999)
Aug 3 Larry Haines [Hecht], American actor (The Odd Couple, Search for Tomorrow), born in Mount Vernon, New York (d. 2008)

Aug 4 Iceberg Slim (a.k.a. Robert Beck), African-American author, born in Chicago, Illinois (d. 1992)

Aug 5 Tom Drake [Alfred Sinclair Alderdice], American actor (Meet Me in St. Louis, Warlock), born in Brooklyn, New York (d. 1982)
Aug 5 Betty Oliphant, Canadian ballerina (d. 2004)

Aug 6 Norman Granz, American record producer (d. 2001)

Aug 7 Cees Buddingh', Dutch poet/writer/interpreter

Aug 9 Robert Aldrich, American director and producer (Dirty Dozen), born in Cranston, Rhode Island (d. 1983)

Aug 10 Eugene Wilkinson, naval officer (first nuclear sub commander), born in Long Beach, California (d. 2013)

Aug 12 Guy Gibson, British aviator, awarded Victoria Cross, born in Simla, India (d. 1944)
Aug 12 Sid Bernstein, music producer/promoter (Beatles, Rolling Stones), born in NYC, New York (d. 2013)

Aug 13 Denis Smallwood, British air chief marshal
Aug 13 Frederick Sanger, British biochemist (Sanger sequencing, Nobel Prize 1958, 1980), born in Rendcomb, Gloucestershire, England (d. 2013)
Aug 13 John Bunting, senior civil servant

Aug 15 Florian Zabach, American musician and TV personality (Hot Canary, Club Embassy), born in Chicago, Illinois
Aug 15 Fay Honey Knopp, American activist (founded a Quaker ministry for men and women in prisons), born in Bridgeport, Connecticut (d. 1995)
Aug 15 Raymond Gallois-Montbrun, composer

Aug 17 Mort Marshall [Mortimer Haig Lichtenstein], American actor (Kiss Me Deadly, Dumplings), born in NYC, New York (d. 1979)
Aug 17 Ike Quebec, American tenor-saxophone player, born in Newark. New Jersey (d. 1963)

Aug 19 James George "Jimmy" Rowles, jazz pianist
Aug 19 Shankar Dayal Sharma, Indian politician, ninth President of India (1992-97), born in Bhopal, British India (d. 1999)

Aug 20 Jacqueline Susann, author (Valley of the Dolls), born in Philadelphia, Pennsylvania (d. 1974)

Aug 21 Billy Reay, Canadian ice hockey player and coach, born in Winnipeg, Manitoba, Canada (d. 2004)

Aug 22 Mary McGrory, American journalist and columnist, born in Roslindale, Boston, Massachusetts (d. 2004)

Aug 24 Ray McIntire, American chemical engineer, born in Gardner, Kansas (d. 1996)
Aug 24 Sikander Bakht, Indian politician, Governor of Kerala, born in Delhi, India (d. 2004)

Aug 25 Leonard Bernstein, American conductor and composer (West Side Story), born in Lawrence, Massachusetts (d. 1990)
Aug 25 Richard Greene, English composer and actor (The Adventures of Robin Hood), born in Plymouth, Devon, England (d. 1985)

Aug 26 Louis W "Louis" Stotijn, bassoonist/conductor (Residence Orchestra)

Aug 27 Lord Winstanley, physician/British MP (Labour)

Aug 28 Alejandro Lanusse, army officer/politician

Aug 29 Jelle Zijlstra, Dutch economist and President of Netherlands Bank (1967-82), born in Oosterbierum, Netherlands (d. 2001)

Aug 30 Ted Williams, American baseball player and last player in MLB to bat over .400 in a single season (Red Sox, AL MVP '46, '49; Trip Crown '42, '47), born in San Diego, California (d. 2002)
Aug 30 Billy Johnson, American baseball player (d. 2006)

Aug 31 Alan Jay Lerner, American lyricist (Lerner & Loewe-My Fair Lady), born in NYC, New York (d. 1986)
Aug 31 Lucrecia Roces Kasilag, composer

September
Sep 2 Allen Drury, author (Advise & Consent-1960 Pulitzer Prize)
Sep 2 Martha Mitchell, wife of Attorney General John Mitchell

Sep 3 Helen Wagner, American actress (Mister Peepers, As The World Turns), born in Lubbock, Texas (d. 2010)

Sep 4 Gerald Wilson, Shelby Miss, orchestra leader (Redd Foxx)
Sep 4 Paul Harvey, American news commentator and radio broadcaster (Rest of the story), born in Tulsa, Oklahoma (d. 2009)
Sep 4 William Talbert, tennis doubles champ (US 1942, 45, 46, 48)

Sep 5 Luis Alcoriza, Mexican screenwriter, film director, and actor, born in Badajoz, Mexico (d. 1992)

Sep 7 Robert Lewis Campbell Lorimer, publisher

Sep 8 Derek Barton, British chemist (Nobel 1969)
Sep 8 John F Seiberling, (Rep-D-OH, 1971-86)

Sep 9 Oscar Luigi Scalfaro, Italian President (1992-99), born in Novara, Italy (d. 2012)

Sep 10 Rin Tin Tin, German shepherd dog (d. 1932)

Sep 11 Donald Blakeslee, American aviator (d. 2008)

Sep 13 Ray Charles, orchestra leader (Perry Como), born in Chicago, Illinois

Sep 14 Jack Somack, American actor (Ball Four, The Frisco Kid, Stockard Channing Show), born in Chicago, Illinois (d. 1983)
Sep 14 Georges Berger, Belgian racing driver (d. 1967)

Sep 15 Nipsey Russell, American comedian (Car 54, Where Are You?), born in Atlanta, Georgia (d. 2005)

Sep 16 Mervyn Pike [Baroness Pike], politician (C), born in Castleford, West Yorkshire (d. 2004)

Sep 17 Chaim Herzog, Israeli president (1983-93), (d. 1997)

Sep 18 John Berger, politician

Sep 20 Margaret "Peg" Phillips, American actress (Northern Exposure, ER, Suddenly Susan), born in Everett, Washington (d. 2002)

Sep 21 Rand Brooks [Arlington Rand Brooks Jr.], American actor (Gone with the Wind, Rin Tin Tin), born in St. Louis, Missouri (d. 2003)

Sep 22 Archibald James Potter, composer
Sep 22 Hans Scholl, German resistance fighter (Die Weisse Rose)
Sep 22 Henryk Szeryng, Zelazowa Wola Poland, violinist (Brahms Concerto)

Sep 24 Audra Lindley, American actress (Three's Company, The Relic, Ropers), born in Los Angeles, California (d. 1997)
Sep 24 Richard Hoggart, author/warden (Goldsmith's College London)

Sep 25 Phil Rizzuto, American sportscaster/shortstop (NY Yankees-MVP 1950), born in Brooklyn, New York

Sep 26 Humphrey van Loo, Dutch news director (ANP/Reuter)

Sep 27 James McCallion, Scottish actor (Coogan's Bluff, Vera Cruz), born in Glasgow, Scotland (d. 1991)
Sep 27 Malcolm Shepherd [2nd Baron Shepherd], Politician (L) and Leader of the House of Lords (1974-76), born in Blackburn, Lancashire (d. 2001)
Sep 27 Martin Ryle, Britain, radio astronomer/astronomer royal (1972-82)

Sep 29 Don Castle, American actor (Born to Speed, Tombstone, Motor Patrol), born in Beaumont, Texas (d. 1966)
Sep 29 Harold Laurence Walters, composer

Sep 30 Lewis Nixon, WWII Veteran (d. 1996)

October
Oct 1 Antonio Iglesias Alvares, composer

Oct 4 Kenichi Fukui, Japanese chemist, Nobel laureate (d. 1998)

Oct 6 André Pilette, Belgian racing driver (d. 1993)

Oct 7 Helmut Dantine, Austrian-American actor (Shadow of the Cloak), born in Vienna, Austria (d. 1982)
Oct 7 Guido Aristarco, film critic
Oct 7 Marcus Klingburg, Israeli soviet spy and epidemiologist

Oct 8 Ron Randell, Australian actor (Loves of Carmen, I am a Camera), born in Sydney, New South Wales (d. 2005)

Oct 9 E Howard Hunt, Hamburg NY, involved in Watergate break-in
Oct 9 Lila Kedrova, Russian-born actress (Zorba the Greek (1964), Sword of the Valiant, The Tenant), born in Petrograd, Russia (d. 2000)

Oct 10 Bobby Byrne, orchestra leader (Club Seven), born in Columbus, Ohio
Oct 10 Jean Gimpel, author/iconoclast
Oct 10 Jigal Allon, Israeli politician

Oct 11 Jerome Robbins, [Rabinowitz], NY, choreographer (Tony-West Side Story)

Oct 12 Emil Cossetto, Croatian composer, born in Trieste, Italy (d. 2006)

Oct 13 Jack MacGowran, Irish actor (King Lear, The Quiet Man, The Exorcist), born in Dublin, Ireland (d. 1973)
Oct 13 Robert Walker, American actor and writer (Strangers on a Train, Bataan, Madame Curie), born in Salt Lake City, Utah (d. 1951)

Oct 14 Doug Ring, cricketer (Australian leggie of the late 40's early 50's)
Oct 14 Marcel Chaput, French Canadian politician (d. 1991)

Oct 16 Bill Nichols, (Rep-D-AL, 1967-)

Oct 17 Rita Hayworth [Margarita Cansino], American actress (Gilda, Cover Girl, The Lady from Shanghai), born in NYC, New York (d. 1987)

Oct 18 Robert "Bobby" Troup, American jazz pianist and actor (Emergency, Acapulco), born in Harrisburg, Pennsylvania (d. 1999)
Oct 18 James Cameron Tudor, politician
Oct 18 Konstantinos Mitsottakis, premier of Greece (1990-)
Oct 18 Willem J "Molly" Geertsema, Dutch liberal/interior minister)
Oct 18 Constantine Mitsotakis [Konstantinos Mitsotakis], Prime Minister of Greece (1990 –1993), born in Halepa, Crete (d. 2017)

Oct 19 Louis Althusser, French philosopher (For Marx, Strangled His Wife)
Oct 19 Robert Charles Evans, mountaineer/doctor

Oct 20 Anton Diffring [Alfred Pollack], German character actor (Assignment Vienna), born in Koblenz, Germany (d. 1989)
Oct 20 Robert Lochner, German journalist (d. 2003)

Oct 22 Lou Klein, American baseball player (d. 1976)

Oct 23 James Daly, American actor (Medical Center, Planet of the Apes), born in Wisconsin Rapids, Wisconsin (d. 1978)
Oct 23 Mary Jeanette "Peggy" Moran, American actress (Double Date, Horror Island), born in Clinton, Iowa (d. 2002)

Oct 27 Paul Dixon, Ohio talk show host (Paul Dixon Show), born in Albia, Iowa (d. 1974)
Oct 27 Teresa Wright, American actress (Eleanor Gehrig-Pride of the Yankees), born in NYC, New York (d. 2005)

Oct 28 Harold Sheperdson, soccer trainer

Oct 29 Bernard Gordon, American writer and producer (d. 2007)

Oct 30 Robert Feller, Van Meter Iowa, MLB pitcher (Cleveland Indians, led AL in strikeouts 7 times)

Oct 31 Ian Stevenson, Canadian-American parapsychologist and reincarnation expert, born in Montreal, Quebec, Canada (d. 2007)

November
Nov 3 Bob Feller, Van Meter, Iowa, American baseball pitcher (Cleveland Indian, 3 no-hitters)
Nov 3 Russell B Long, (Sen-D-LA, 1948-86)
Nov 3 Elizabeth P. Hoisington, American Brigadier General (d. 2007)
Nov 3 Dean Riesner, film and television screenwriter (d. 2002)

Nov 4 Art Carney, American actor (Ed Norton-Honeymooners), born in Mount Vernon, New York (d. 2003)
Nov 4 Cameron Mitchell, American actor (The High Chaparral), born in Dallastown, Pennsylvania (d. 1994)

Nov 6 Ronnie Brody, British actor (Superman 3, What's Up Nurse, Ritz), born in Bristol, England (d. 1991)

Nov 7 Billy Graham, American Baptist evangelist (Crusades) described as 1 of the 20th century's most influential Christian leaders, born in Charlotte, North Carolina (d. 2018)
Nov 7 Maria Teresa de Noronha, Portuguese Fado singer (d. 1993)
Nov 7 Paul Aussaresses, French general

Nov 8 Hermann Zapf, German typeface designer (Palatino and Optima), born in Nuremberg (d. 2015)

Nov 9 Howard Shanet, American conductor (Night of the Tropics), born in Brooklyn, New York (d. 2006)
Nov 9 Spiro Agnew, American politician (Vice President, 1969 until resignation over corruption allegations in 1973), born in Baltimore, Maryland (d. 1996)

Nov 9 Choi Hong Hi, South Korean army general and Founder of Taekwon-Do, born in Hwadae, Myongchon County, North Hamgyong Province, Japanese Korea (d. 2002)
Nov 9 Thomas Ferebee, Enola Gay bombardier over Hiroshima, born in Mocksville, North Carolina (d. 2000)

Nov 10 Ernst Fischer, German chemist (Nobel 1973), born in Munich, Germany (d. 2007)
Nov 10 Jack McCoy, TV host (Live Like a Millionaire), born in Akron, Ohio
Nov 10 Martin Hanley, South African cricketer (took 1-88 with off-spin in Test for South Africa), born in Aliwal North, Cape Province (d. 2000)
Nov 10 Oda Blinder, [Yolanda Corsen], Antillean poetess (Doorstep)

Nov 11 Jürg Baur, German composer, born in Düsseldorf (d. 2010)
Nov 11 Stubby Kaye [Bernard Solomon Kotzin], American actor (Guys & Dolls, Lil' Abner, Cat Ballou), born in NYC, New York (d. 1997)

Nov 13 Janine Andrade, French violinist, born in Besançon, France (d. 1997)

Nov 18 Tasker Watkins, Welsh World War II hero (d. 2007)

Nov 19 Catherine Elizabeth Pennington, personal assistant
Nov 19 Hendrik Christoffel Van de Hulst, Utrecht the Netherlands, Dutch astronomer who correctly predicted the existence of the 21 cm hyper-fine line of neutral atomic hydrogen in interstellar space

Nov 20 Dora Ratjen, German man possing as woman high jumper (Olympic 4th 1936)

Nov 22 Claiborne Pell, (Sen-D-RI, 1961-)

Nov 24 Roley Jenkins, cricketer (English leg-spinner 1948-52)
Nov 24 Captain Stubby [Tom Fouts], American author and comedian

(Captain Stubby and the Buccaneers), born in Carroll County, Indiana (d. 2004)
Nov 24 William Strethan "Wild Bill" Davis, musician

Nov 26 Patricio Aylwin, Chilean lawyer and politician, President of Chile (1990-94), born in Viña del Mar, Chile (d. 2016)

Nov 27 Zeev Wolfgang Steinberg, composer

Nov 29 Herb Shriner, host/humorist (Herb Shriner Show), born in Toledo, Ohio
Nov 29 Madeleine L'Engle, [Franklin], American sci-fi author (Ilsa, Love Letters)

Nov 30 Efren Zimbalist Jr, American actor (77 Sunset Strip, FBI, Scruples), born in NYC, New York (d. 2014)

December
Dec 1 Kirby Laing, English contractor/multi-millionaire

Dec 2 Milton Delugg, orchestra leader (Tonight Show), born in Los Angeles, California

Dec 3 Abdul Haris Nasution, Indonesian general (d. 2000)

Dec 6 Granville James Leveson Gower, land owner
Dec 6 Harold Horace Hopkins, inventor (Endoscope)
Dec 6 Peter A Juten, office clerk/resistance fighter
Dec 6 Willem Oosterheers, resistance fighter

Dec 7 Jorunn Vidar, composer

Dec 8 Ian Johnson, cricketer (Australian Test captbetween Hassett & Craig)
Dec 8 Gérard Souzay, French baritone (d. 2004)

Dec 9 Jerome Beatty Jr., American author

Dec 10 Anne Gwynne [Marguerite Gwynne Trice], American model and actress (Ride 'em Cowboy, House of Frankenstein), born in Waco, Texas (d. 2003)
Dec 10 Anatoli Tarasov, Russian ice hockey coach (d. 1995)

Dec 11 Aleksandr Solzhenitsyn, Russian writer (Cancer Ward, Nobel 1970), born in Kislovodsk, Russia (d. 2008)

Dec 12 Joe Williams [Joseph Goreed], Cordele, Georgia, American jazz singer (Everyday I have the Blues)
Dec 12 Nilda Pinto, [NM Geerdink-Jesurun P], Curacao writer (Nanzi)

Dec 14 James T. Aubrey, American television executive (d. 1994)
Dec 14 B.K.S. Iyengar, Indian yoga advocate

Dec 15 Jeff Chandler [Ira Grossel], American actor (Broken Arrow), born in Brooklyn, New York (d. 1961)

Dec 16 Henry Clarke, fashion photographer
Dec 16 Pierre Delanoë, French songwriter and lyricist (d. 2006)

Dec 19 Professor Longhair [Henry Roeland Byrd], American blues singer and pianist, born in Bogalusa, Louisiana (d. 1980)

Dec 21 Donald Regan, White House staffer/US Secretary of Treasury (1981-85)
Dec 21 Kurt Waldheim, Austrian 4th Secretary-General of the United Nations (1972-81) and 9th President of Austria (1986-92), born in Sankt Andrä-Wördern, Austria (d. 2007)

Dec 22 Frankie Darro [Frank Johnson], American actor (Radio Ranch, Wild Boys of the Road, Valley of Wanted Men), born in Chicago, Illinois (d. 1976)

Dec 22 William Kennedy, baseball player

Dec 23 Helmut Schmidt, Chancellor of West Germany (SPD, 1974- 82), born in Hamburg (d. 2015)
Dec 23 Jose Greco, Italian flamenco dancer (Holiday for Lovers)
Dec 23 Kumar Pallana, Indian character actor and vaudevillian (Bottle Rocket, Rushmore), born in Indore, India (d. 2013)

Dec 25 Anwar Sadat, 3rd President of Egypt (1970-81, Nobel 1978), born in Monufia, Egypt (d. 1981)
Dec 25 Eddie Safranski, orchestra leader (Jonathan Winters Show), born in Pittsburgh, Pennsylvania
Dec 25 Ahmed Ben Bella, Maghnia, Algeria, politician, first President of Algeria, (d. 2012)

Dec 26 George Rallis, Greek politician, Prime Minister of Greece (d. 2006)

Dec 27 John Celardo, American comic strip artist

Dec 30 W Eugene Smith, US photographer (Saipan, Walk to Paradise Garden)

Famous Deaths
January
Jan 2 Sijbe K Bakker, vicar/theologist (Christian-Socialism), dies at 42

Jan 6 Georg F L P Cantor, German mathematician: collection, dies at 72

Jan 8 Michael Hertz, composer, dies at 73

Jan 8 Ellis H. Roberts, American politician (b. 1827)

Jan 9 Émile Reynaud, French scientist (b. 1844)

Jan 18 Bohuslav Jeremiáš, Czech composer, dies at 58

Jan 24 George Arthur Crump, Founder of the Pine Valley Golf Club in Clementon NJ (b. 1871)

Jan 28 John McCrae, Canadian poet/physician/soldier, dies of pneumonia at 45

February
Feb 2 John L Sullivan, Mass, heavyweight boxing champ, dies at 59

Feb 6 Gustav Klimt, Austrian painter/cartoonist, dies at 55

Feb 7 Alexander Sergeyevich Taneyev, Russian composer, dies at 68

Feb 9 Emiel van der Straeten, [Delrue], Flemish playwright, dies at 30

Feb 10 Abdul Hamid II Ottoman Sultan (b. 1842)
Feb 10 Ernesto Teodoro Moneta, Italian pacifist, Nobel Prize Laureate, dies at 84

Feb 17 Wilfrid Laurier, 7th Prime Minister of Canada (Liberal: 1896-1911), dies of a stroke at 76

March

Mar 1 Johan Gustaf Emil Sjogren, composer, dies at 64

Mar 2 Hubert Howe Bancroft, American historian, ethnologist (History of Pacific States), dies at 85

Mar 4 Eugene D'Harcourt, composer, dies at 58

Mar 9 [Benjamin] Franc[lin] Wedekind, German writer/press sec, dies at 53

Mar 10 Jim McCormick, Scottish-born American baseball player, dies at 61

Mar 13 Karel Stecker, composer, dies at 57

Mar 15 Jose Silvestre de los Dolores White Lafitte, composer, dies at 82
Mar 15 Juliette Marie Olga Lili Boulanger, composer, dies at 24
Mar 15 Lili Boulanger, composer, dies at 24
Mar 15 George Alexander [Samson], British actor, theatre producer and manager, dies at 59

Mar 18 Willem Coenen, composer, dies at 80

Mar 19 Willem H de Beaufort, Dutch historian/liberal politician, dies at 73

Mar 20 Lewis A. Grant, American Civil War General (b. 1828)

Mar 23 Cesar Cortinas, composer, dies at 27

Mar 24 Théophile "Théo" Ysaÿe, Belgian composer and pianist, dies at 53

Mar 25 Claude Debussy, French composer (Iberia/La Mer), dies in Paris at 55

Mar 26 Caesar A Cui, Lithuanian fort builder/composer, dies at 83

April
Apr 1 Karl Fritjof Valentin, composer, dies at 64

Apr 5 Paul Vidal de la Blanche, French geographer, dies at 73

Apr 11 Arthur Ochse, cricketer (WW I played for South Africa in 1889 aged 19), dies

Apr 13 Lavr Georgevich Kornilov, Russian general (b. 1870)

Apr 20 Reginald Harry Mybirgh Hands, cricketer (1 Test for SA), dies

Apr 21 Manfred von Richthofen [The Red Baron], German World War I fighter ace, dies at 25 after his plane is shot down

Apr 23 Percy Thomson Dean, lt-commander, killed at Zeebrugge, dies

Apr 28 Gavrilo Princip, Bosnian-Serb assassin of Archduke Ferdinand, dies at 23

May
May 3 Charlie Soong, Chinese Methodist missionary and key player in the Xinhai Revolution of 1911, dies at 55

May 9 George Coşbuc, Romanian poet (b. 1866)

May 12 Abel Hoadley, Australian confectioner (Violet Crumble), dies at 73

May 14 James Gordon Bennett, Jr., American newspaper publisher (b. 1841)

May 16 Eusapia Palladino, Italian spiritual medium, dies at 64

May 18 Toivo Kuula, Finnish composer, dies after being shot in a quarrel at 34

May 19 Gervais Raoul Lufbery, French-American World War I fighter pilot and flying ace, dies at 33

May 24 Evan Williams, American oratorio tenor

May 27 Henry Adams, US literature historian (Esther), dies at 80

May 30 Georgi V Plechanov, Russian revolutionary theorist, dies

June
Jun 1 Friedrich Richard Faltin, composer, dies at 83
Jun 1 Jaroslav Novotny, Czech composer, dies at 32

Jun 10 Arrigio Enrico Boito, composer, dies at 76

Jun 17 Derek Barber, CEO (Countryside Commission), dies

Jun 25 Jake Beckley, American baseball player, dies at 50

Jun 26 Peter Rosegger, Austrian poet and Nobel Prize laureate, dies at 74

July
Jul 2 Mohammed V Resjad, sultan of Turkey (1909-18), dies

Jul 3 Sultan Mehmed V of the Ottoman Empire (b. 1844)
Jul 3 David Alfred Thomas, 1st Viscount Rhondda, Welsh coal-mining entrepreneur, dies at 62

Jul 6 Count von Mirbach, German ambassador to Moscow, dies

Jul 12 Dragutin Lerman, Croatian explorer, dies at 54

Jul 17 Alexei Nikolaevich, last Tsarevich of Russia and son of Tsar Nicholas II, executed at 13
Jul 17 Alexandra Feodorovna, German-born Russian empress wife of Tsar Nicholas II, executed at 46
Jul 17 Anastasia Nikolaevna, Russian grand duchess and daughter of Tsar Nicholas II, executed at 17
Jul 17 Eugene Botkin, Russian court physician of Tsar Nicholas II, executed at 53
Jul 17 Ivan Kharitonov, Russian cook of Tsar Nicholas II, executed around the age of 46
Jul 17 Anna Demidova, Russian lady in waiting of Tsarina Alexandra, executed at 40
Jul 17 Maria Nikolaevna, Russian grand duchess and daughter of Tsar Nicholas II, executed at 19
Jul 17 Nicholas II, last Tsar of Russia (1894-1917), executed at 50
Jul 17 Olga Nikolaevna, Russian grand duchess and daughter of Tsar Nicholas II, executed at 22
Jul 17 Tatiana Nikolaevna, Russian grand duchess and daughter of Tsar Nicholas II, executed at 21
Jul 17 Alexei Trupp, Russian footman and assistant of Tsar Nicholas II, executed at 62

Jul 18 Grand Duchess Elizabeth Fyodorovna (b. 1864)

Jul 19 Joost van Vollenhoven, Neth, gov-gen (French West-Africa), dies

Jul 22 Indra Lal Roy, Indian pilot (b. 1898)

Jul 25 Carlos Guido y Spano, Argentine poet (Mexico, canto epico), dies
Jul 25 Franiska zu Reventlow, writer, dies at 47

Jul 26 Eduard "Mick" Mannock, British WW I flyer (Victoria Cross), dies

Jul 29 Ernest William Christmas, Australian painter (b. 1863)

Jul 30 Chaim Soloveitchik, Rabbi of Brisk, talmudic scholar, dies
Jul 30 Joyce Kilmer, American poet, dies at 31

August
Aug 1 John Riley Banister, American cowboy and Texas Ranger (b. 1854)

Aug 3 Albert P Hahn, Dutch political cartoonist (Het Volk), dies at 41

Aug 8 Gertrude E Durden Rush, US composer/playwright, dies at 38

Aug 10 Erich Lowenhardt, Germany flying ace of World War I (b. 1897)

Aug 12 Anna Held, Polish-born French actress and singer (A Parisian Model), dies of cancer at 46

Aug 15 Heinrich Köselitz [Peter Gast], German composer, dies at 64

Aug 22 Korbinian Brodmann, German neurologist (b. 1868)

Aug 29 Max Dauthendey, writer, dies at 51

Aug 31 Joe English, Irish/Flemish signaler (WWI), dies at 36

September
Sep 3 Fanya Kaplan, Russian who shot at Lenin on Aug 30th, executed

Sep 4 Max Dauthendy, German painter/author (Raubmenschen), dies at 51)

Sep 12 George Reid, fourth Prime Minister of Australia (b. 1845)

Sep 18 Ernest Bristow Farrar, composer, dies at 33

Sep 19 Liza Nina Mary Frederica Lehmann, composer, dies at 56

Sep 25 John Ireland, Irish-American archbishop of St Paul (1888-1918), dies at 80
Sep 25 Mikhail Alekseev, Russian general (b. 1857)

Sep 28 Georg Simmel, German sociologist and philosopher (b. 1858)
Sep 28 Freddie Stowers, American soldier (b. 1896)

October
Oct 5 Roland Garros, French stunt flyer, dies

Oct 7 Hubert Parry, English musicologist and composer (Jerusalem), dies at 70

Oct 9 Michail V Alekseyev, Russian general (WWI), murdered at 60

Oct 13 Gerrit Engelke, German writer (Briefer der Liebe), dies

Oct 15 Sai Baba of Shirdi, Indian saint (b. circa 1838)

Oct 16 Felix Arndt, American composer, dies during the Spanish Flu pandemic at 29

Oct 17 Gordon White, cricketer (WW I Superb South African batsman 1905-12), dies

Oct 19 Joseph Lesage, French painter/etcher (WWI), dies at 34
Oct 19 Harold Lockwood, American actor (Tess of the Storm Country), dies from the flu at 31

Oct 22 Myrtle Gonzalez, American actress regarded as Hollywood's first Latin and Hispanic movie star actress (Missy, Her Great Part), dies from influenza and heart ailment at 27

Oct 24 Alexander Charles Lecocq, composer, dies at 86

Oct 28 Ulisse Dini, Italian mathematician (b. 1845)
Oct 28 Edward Bouchet, American Physicist, 1st African American to receive US Ph.D, dies at 66

Oct 31 Egon Schiele, Austria painter/graphic artist, dies at 28
Oct 31 Stephen Tisza, Hungarian PM (-1917), assassinated by soldiers

November
Nov 3 Aleksandr Mikhailovich Lyapunov, Russian scientist (b. 1857)

Nov 4 Wilfred Owens, anti-war poet (Anthem for doomed youth), dies at 25
Nov 4 Andrew Dickson White, American historian and educator, 1st President of Cornell University, dies at 85

Nov 9 Guillaume Apollinaire, [Kostrowitsky], Fr poet (Alcools), dies at 38

Nov 11 Victor Adler, Austrian neurologist/foreign minister, dies
Nov 11 George Lawrence Price, Canadian soldier, last person to be killed in WW I (b. 1892)

Nov 13 Marten Baersma, [MH Bottema], Fries author, dies at 28

Nov 15 Georges Antoine, composer, dies at 26

Nov 18 Reggie Schwartz, cricketer (55 wickets for South Africa), dies

Nov 26 Charlie McLeod, cricketer (all-rounder for Australia 1894-1905), dies

Nov 28 Alexis Contant, composer, dies at 60

Nov 29 Harald Kidde, Danish writer (Helten), dies at 40

December
Dec 2 Margit Kaffka, Hungarian writer, dies in the flu pandemic at 38
Dec 2 Edmond Rostand, French poet and dramatist (b. 1868)

Dec 11 Ivan Cankar, Slavic author (Hlapec Jernej), dies at 42

Dec 14 Sidonio Pais, prince of Portugal, murdered

Dec 18 Henryk Jarecki, composer, dies at 72

Dec 22 Albijn van de Abeele, Flemish author/mayor/painter, dies at 83

Dec 26 Bertram Luard-Selby, composer, dies at 65

Dec 28 George H White, last post Reconstruction congressman (Penn), dies
Dec 28 Olavo Bilac, Brazilian poet (b. 1865)

1918 Fun Facts

Top Ten Baby Names of 1918: Mary, Helen, Dorothy, Margaret, Ruth, John, William, James, Robert, Charles

US Life Expectancy: (1918) Males: 36.6 years, Females: 42.2 years

Opha Mae Johnson became the first woman allowed to join the US Marine Corps.

In Russia, the day after January 31st was February 14th, not February 1st – that's the day Russia transitioned from the Julian to the Gregorian calendar.

When Manfred von Richtofen (the Red Baron) was shot down and killed in 1918, the British Army gave him a full military funeral, complete with clergy, a gun salute and a wreath inscribed with, "To Our Gallant and Worthy Foe."

Nobel Prize Winners:
Physics – Max Karl Ernst Ludwig Planck
Chemistry – Fritz Haber
Medicine – not awarded
Literature – not awarded
Peace – not awarded

Sports:
World Series Champions: Boston Red Sox
Stanley Cup Champs: Toronto Arenas
U.S. Open Golf: not held (WWI)
U.S. Tennis (Men/Ladies): Robert Lindley Murray/Molla Bjurstedt
Wimbledon (Men/Women): not held (WWI)
NCAA Football Champions: Pitt & Michigan
Kentucky Derby Winner: Exterminator
Boston Marathon Winner: Camp Devens relay team Time: 2:29:53

1918 Calendar

1918 CALENDAR

January

	Sun	Mon	Tue	Wed	Thu	Fri	Sat
1			1	2	3	4	5
2	6	7	8	9	10	11	12
3	13	14	15	16	17	18	19
4	20	21	22	23	24	25	26
5	27	28	29	30	31		

February

	Sun	Mon	Tue	Wed	Thu	Fri	Sat
5						1	2
6	3	4	5	6	7	8	9
7	10	11	12	13	14	15	16
8	17	18	19	20	21	22	23
9	24	25	26	27	28		

March

	Sun	Mon	Tue	Wed	Thu	Fri	Sat
9						1	2
10	3	4	5	6	7	8	9
11	10	11	12	13	14	15	16
12	17	18	19	20	21	22	23
13	24	25	26	27	28	29	30
14	31						

April

	Sun	Mon	Tue	Wed	Thu	Fri	Sat
14		1	2	3	4	5	6
15	7	8	9	10	11	12	13
16	14	15	16	17	18	19	20
17	21	22	23	24	25	26	27
18	28	29	30				

May

	Sun	Mon	Tue	Wed	Thu	Fri	Sat
18				1	2	3	4
19	5	6	7	8	9	10	11
20	12	13	14	15	16	17	18
21	19	20	21	22	23	24	25
22	26	27	28	29	30	31	

June

	Sun	Mon	Tue	Wed	Thu	Fri	Sat
22							1
23	2	3	4	5	6	7	8
24	9	10	11	12	13	14	15
25	16	17	18	19	20	21	22
26	23	24	25	26	27	28	29
27	30						

July

	Sun	Mon	Tue	Wed	Thu	Fri	Sat
27		1	2	3	4	5	6
28	7	8	9	10	11	12	13
29	14	15	16	17	18	19	20
30	21	22	23	24	25	26	27
31	28	29	30	31			

August

	Sun	Mon	Tue	Wed	Thu	Fri	Sat
31					1	2	3
32	4	5	6	7	8	9	10
33	11	12	13	14	15	16	17
34	18	19	20	21	22	23	24
35	25	26	27	28	29	30	31

Setptember

	Sun	Mon	Tue	Wed	Thu	Fri	Sat
36	1	2	3	4	5	6	7
37	8	9	10	11	12	13	14
38	15	16	17	18	19	20	21
39	22	23	24	25	26	27	28
40	29	30					

October

	Sun	Mon	Tue	Wed	Thu	Fri	Sat
40		1	2	3	4	5	
41	6	7	8	9	10	11	12
42	13	14	15	16	17	18	19
43	20	21	22	23	24	25	26
44	27	28	29	30	31		

November

	Sun	Mon	Tue	Wed	Thu	Fri	Sat
44						1	2
45	3	4	5	6	7	8	9
46	10	11	12	13	14	15	16
47	17	18	19	20	21	22	23
48	24	25	26	27	28	29	30

December

	Sun	Mon	Tue	Wed	Thu	Fri	Sat
49	1	2	3	4	5	6	7
50	8	9	10	11	12	13	14
51	15	16	17	18	19	20	21
52	22	23	24	25	26	27	28
53	29	30	31				

Look out for more books in the Series by Kerry Butters.

www.ingramcontent.com/pod-product-compliance
Lightning Source LLC
Chambersburg PA
CBHW071115280526
45787CB00003B/1055